Make no mistake about it – enlightenment is a destructive process. Enlightenment is the crumbling away of untruth; it's seeing through the façade of pretense. It's the complete eradication of everything we imagined to be true.

A·WAK·EN·ING

Noun - awakening; plural noun: awakenings

An act or moment of becoming suddenly aware of something, an act of waking from sleep, the beginning or rousing of something.

Adjective - awakening

coming into existence or awareness.

Most of the so called African Americans are unaware of their true identity. We will present information to show you how we are sleep walking through this life and why it is critical for us to wake up in order to fulfill the prophecy and destiny God set before the creation of the world. Let us take a deeper dive into the awakening. There have been actual incidents of people walking, talking, and eating, all while they sleep. It is possible to be still asleep and look like you are awake, but you are not.

Contents

God has a plan and He is working His plan.

This is going to be a journey from the first man Adam to YOU. God pressed this message upon us and we want to thank you in advance for coming on this journey with us. Be present, attentive, and open to the workings of the Holy Spirit. **We are not experts** in this area of study, and we do not have all the answers, but we do have some of the questions to begin the dialog. The time is upon us to **wake up** sleeping Giants! These sessions will challenge your beliefs, they will produce uncomfortable feelings and have you questioning what you thought you knew. Just agree to be open to information and allow the Holy Spirit to help you discern truth as it relates to you.

The TRUTH is the TRUTH, even if no one believes it, and a LIE is a LIE even if everyone believes it.

Racism is taught behavior that is passed down from generation to generation. Our likes and dislikes, our love and hates, our beliefs that some people are above, equal to or beneath us (inferior to us). Therefore, they are treated differently, and it influences every area of our lives. Racism is systemic and embedded in all of our society's institutions (Government, Education, Entertainment, Financing (banking and wall street); it runs deep in our culture! This is not a hate message; it is a truth message. We invite the Holy Spirit to have His way and reveal truth. We believe that the Holy Spirit indwells, guides, teaches, convicts, intercedes, enables, and unifies.

Have we been miss-educated?

We all believe it is so important to get educated, right? We make sure our kids go to school, but how many of us put that same importance on Biblical study? We have our priorities twisted, we say God is the most important Person in our lives but do our actions prove that fact?

> "The beginning of wisdom is this; get wisdom, though it cost all you have, get understanding." **Proverbs 4:7**

> "Study to show thyself approved unto God, a workman that need not to be ashamed but rightly dividing the word of truth." **2Timothy 2:15**

The Mis-Education of the Negro written by Carter G. Woodson tells us that, "when you control a man's thinking, you do not have to worry about his actions. You do not have to tell him to stand here or go yonder. He will find his "proper place" and will stay in it. You do not need to send him to the back door, he will go without being told. In fact, if there is no back door, he will cut one for his special benefit. His education makes it necessary."

QUESTIONS THAT PLAGUE AFRICAN AMERICANS

- WHO AMI?
- WHO WAS I BEFORE SLAVERY?
- WHERE IS MY ORIGIN?
- WHAT IS MY NATIONALITY?
- WHY AM I HERE?
- WHERE AM I GOING?

All of us should know the answers to these basic questions. All other races can answer these questions with the exception of the African American race. Our nationality is not black, that is a color. We look upon Africa as an uneducated, savage place and that was done by design, so that you would not relate to it or identify with the culture.

I saw a video of this young man asking a group of young black boys and girls about different nationalities and their country of origin. He said "Chinese" and the group replied "China". He said "Italians" and the group replied "Italy," Brazilians-Brazil, Cubans-Cuba, Egyptians-Egypt, and so on. Then he said "African Americans" and they were silent... Let that sink in for a minute. They knew of every country of origin except their own. Why is that? Why do they continue to rename us? We have been known by so many names (Coon, Nigger, Black, Negro, African, African American).

Since the Bible is a prophetic book, where is the prophecy about the Trans-Atlantic Slave Trade? That is truly one of the greatest devastating events to happened to a people. Where was God? Did that catch Him by surprise? We will look into Scripture for answers to see that not only was the Trans-Atlantic Slave Trade prophesied, it was prophesied by the Prophets, Moses and Christ.

Our history has been hidden and great lengths have been taken to keep it from us until such a time as this. Are we awakening now that God is revealing the truth? Is it coincidental that we are embracing our natural beauty, our hair styles, our thick lips and hips, our love of self?

It's time for the AWAKENING!!!!!

Prior to the Trans-Atlantic Slave Trade in the 1600s, what was your nationality? What did you call yourself? Was it African? Africa is a continent, and that continent is comprised of 53 different countries. Which one do you come from? What language did you speak? There are over 1500 dialects spoken in Africa. What clothing did you wear? What food did you eat? What religion did you practice? Who was your God? Most African Americans do not know the answers to these questions and have no remembrance of any history prior to the Trans-Atlantic Slave Trade. Is that by coincidence or random chance? Have you ever asked yourself why is it in the public school system that every time the subject of black history is taught, it ALWAYS begins in 1619 with slavery? Why is that? Why are the schools so committed to revolving black history to the last 400 years? Is it because there is not any historical data prior to the 1600s? What is so secretive, what's the big deal, and why can't our history be taught 100 years before slavery, 200, 300? Do any of these questions cause you to go "hum"???? Billions of dollars have been spent to keep our history from us, but historians, biblical scholars, and archeologist know something most of us do not know and that is, we do not know our true identify.

We used the Holy Bible as our Primary source and Biblical Commentaries. We also used YouTube videos and the latest scientific discoveries and resources. Although it is not mandatory to include the videos, we feel the videos will aid in your understanding as well as provide a visual of several of the truths being reveled in these sessions. A picture is worth a thousand words so with that being said, an internet connection, such as a cell phone, laptop or pc as a viewing method will be required.

We will reference the book of Enoch and the Apocrypha/1ˢᵗ Maccabees and other non-canalized books as they are referenced in the Bible. It is referenced in the Bible itself; therefore, we have viewed it as a credible source.

For example, look at the book of Esther. It ends at chapter ten verse three. Did you ever wonder why that chapter only has three verses? Are there more?

Current Day Version   1611 Version

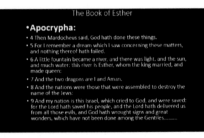

YES, look in a 1611 King James Version of the Bible, you will find Esther, and it starts at chapter ten verse four. (See copy of the Apocrypha).

STATEMENTS TO PONDER

- This is not black theology. It is not about a race of people. It is about a nation of people.
- Color doesn't matter but Nationality does. God is not a respecter of person but He is a respecter of purpose.

- History can be a set of lies agreed upon.
- Racism is prejudice plus power.
- When a lie is all that is known then the truth is inconceivable. The things that we believe become our truth.
- When you tell a big enough lie and tell it frequently enough (books, tv and movies), it will be believed.
- NO Condemnation before investigation. You should never resist what you haven't investigated. Always be open to examine your own belief system to receive new information because no one knows it all.
- Truth is more important than comfort.
- Those who believe a lie have become ignorant of the truth.
- We need a paradigm shift. A change in our intellectual perception of view of how things work in the world.

There are so many things that we need to consider. These statements are just that; thoughts we would like you to consider as you begin this journey.

TRUTH OR DECEPTION

Truth – The real facts about something; not what you've been told, shown or believe, but it is the REAL DEAL.

Deception - A lie that is made to seem like the truth. Webster defines deception as the act of making someone believe something that is not true. The act of deceiving someone. **(Brain washing)**

Ignorance – The lack of knowledge, understanding, or education; the state of being ignorant.

It is not your fault if someone is teaching you a lie, but it does become your fault if you accept the lie and do not seek truth yourself. The Bible tells us that we must study ourselves!!!

Next, we will see a video entitled, "The Monkey Business Illusion." <u>**Concentrate on counting the number of passes that the team in white shirts make!**</u> This will show how things can be in plain sight, yet we miss them!

If this video link is no longer available, search by the video name.
(View this YouTube video link) https://youtu.be/IGQmdoK_ZfY

How many times did the white shirts pass the ball? How many people saw the monkey? Why did you miss him? If you saw the monkey, did you notice the other changes? (one player left and the curtain changed from red to yellow).

A lot of the information that we will be going through has been in plain view our entire lives, but we have not seen it. We have had hundreds of years of conditioning so that we would not see truth, even the obvious, we accepted excuses without researching for ourselves. It was like the monkey in the room or the curtain changing, we missed it or saw some of it, but not everything. God is allowing truth to be revealed. He is allowing us to see more and more of what has been in plain sight all the time.

Have we, as a people, missed who we are when it has been in plain sight in God's Word and History? If so, why?

> *"Be not conformed to this world but be ye transformed by the renewing of your mind that you may prove what is that good, and acceptable and perfect will of God."* **Romans 12:2**

In order to renew our minds, we will have to peel back layers of untruth. We will have to re-learn certain things about History and Biology. Science is always trying to disprove the Bible but it ends up proving the Bible.

Session One is all about perception. How do you perceive your History, Present and Future? All perception is based on ones' experiences, beliefs and prejudices.

Webster defines perception as;
"the ability to see, hear, or become aware of something through the senses."

Introduction
Purpose
Matrix Red Pill or Blue Pill
The Doll Test/Break Out Groups
Objectives
What is the Bible?
What is History?

Session 1

INTRODUCTION

This study will consist of six sessions designed to uncover truth that we believe will create a hunger for knowledge and a zeal to know more about who we are as a people. We must embrace this opportunity to rally together under the umbrella of the Universal Church of Yeshua (Jesus Christ) recognizing the true enemy and collectively learn to love, understand and accept each other as brothers and sisters in Christ. Our prayer is that each of you will take this life changing information and begin to walk passionately and effectively in truth not deception and share with others in order that we as a people will know our true identity.

It appears that every nationality of people knows their origin, their heritage, their nationality except us. That must change. With all the technology available to us; there are no excuses for not knowing. **It is imperative that we know in order to fulfill our destiny in prophecy**.

We have to learn what our **Messiah's name** is. How can we call on a God, and we don't even know what His name is? We can no longer operate in a victim mentality. We must take hold of God's word and operate in His promises about His chosen people.

Lastly, once **you know better, you do better** and will not keep silent but share this information with others. **Tell Others!**

PURPOSE

God has allowed a deep sleep to over take His people because of disobedience. This is the place, time and generation to reveal His truth. We will NOT continue to accept business as ususal, but be an agent of change to expose the true identity of the people in the bible and the purpose of the biblical Hebrew Israelites.

We all will experience not only spiritual freedom but physical, mental, economic and social freedoms. Instead of living under the curse, we will be free to begin to experience God's blessings as we live out His purpose.

Do you wonder why there seems to be so much adversity now, all of the unrest in the Middle East, so many unjustified shootings and the community coming together to bring awareness to these issues? Do you think all of this is coincidental that so many of our women are beginning to embrace their natural beauty by wearing their natural hair? I submit to you that there is an awakening happening before our very eyes and you are a part of it. As subtle as it may seem, **God is awakening His people**! I truly believe God has drawn you to this book to allow you to have a clearer vision of His plan for your life. While America and Christianity is on the decline, God is raising up His chosen people.

Next, we will see a video entitled, "The Matrix Red Pill or Blue Pill." This will show how each of us have the right to know the truth, but will we choose it?

THE MATRIX – RED PILL OR BLUE PILL

If this video link is no longer available, search by the video name.
(View this YouTube video link) https://youtu.be/zE7PKRjrid4

Morpheus asked Neon to choose between the blue and the red pill. Take the blue pill and you will continue in your dream world or take the red pill and you will wake up and see/experience true reality. Are you ready to take the RED pill?

> *If my people, which are called by my name, shall humble themselves, and pray, and seek my face, and turn from their wicked ways; then will I hear from heaven, and will forgive their sin, and will heal their land.* 2nd **Chronicles 7:14**

When we think about our children, would you agree that our children are messages that we send into the future? With that being said, what message are we sending? Why is it so important for us to understand where we are as a people? So that we can get in line with God's word to fulfill our destiny! We feel this video will help you understand the current state of the society.

The next video is a study entitled, **"The Doll Test."** This video is a recreation from the original study done during integration. Please pay close attention to each response. This video will show the more things change, the more they stay the same.

THE DOLL TEST

If this video link is no longer available, search by the video name. (View this YouTube video link) https://youtu.be/fzUqyKX5bMk

What stood out to you in the video clip? How do you feel about what you saw? Why do you think the children answered like they did? What can we do to change this perspective? Why did two – thirds of the children in this test respond positively toward the lighter skin dolls and negatively toward the darker skin dolls? We have been taught regardless of color, religion, economic or sociological background, that white is right. Why does this lie continue to fester so that one group of people think they are superior and another group of people think they are inferior because of the amount or lack of melanin in skin?

OBJECTIVES

- Enlightenment to the true identity of "The Biblical Hebrew Israelites", God chosen people.
- Expose the historical and continued deception of Satan.
- Reveal the Bible as a History book about people of color.
- Inspire and motivate to continue seeking out truth.
- Understand the curse of Deuteronomy 28 and its correlation to the plight of the African American.
- Expand the understanding of the biblical genealogy from Adam to Jesus.
- Create a greater appreciation for the Mother Land "Africa".
- Identify racial prejudice and its role in biblical distortion.
- Explore the plight of the Hebrew Israelites and the scattering of the tribe of Juda.

What is the Bible? It is a book written by inspired men of God that reflects God's activity in the world with man and man's responsibility to man and man's responsibility to God. In other words, it is a book containing the revelation of God to man and His acts of redeeming love.

African history, European history, and the Bible all give proof to the fact that civilization began in Africa, where the black nations, including the black Hebrew people, were the original inhabitants. Moreover, the real truth has been grossly neglected, suppressed, distorted and flavored with racial prejudice. What does racial prejudice mean? (Those who are in control and have the power to influence negatively the outcome of others.)

The Bible is the original history of the Hebrew-Israelites. We have been looking at the Bible wrong. It is not their history book but the truth is, it is OUR history book.

What is History? Webster defines history as, the study of past events; events of the past; past events that relate to a particular subject, place, organization, etc. History is written from a person's personal perspective and experiences, beliefs and motives. Can history be distorted by a writer's perspective, experiences, beliefs and motives?

Those who have the ability to write/document history have been known to write from their perspective slanting history to fit their purpose. We normally take whatever is in writing as gospel (not to mention, TV and movies). Perception may be different based on the person telling the story.

Next, we will see a video entitled, "A Time To Kill." The video picks up during the closing arguments of a murder trial. It shows how it is very difficult for us to see from others perspective, but it is possible if you look with the right lens.

TIME TO KILL CLOSING ARGUMENT

If this video link is no longer available, search by the video name.
(View this YouTube video link) https://youtu.be/He1PDqzCAgg

What is the attorney able to accomplish? He wanted them to see the victim as "WHITE" WHY? How do you see you? How do you see others? Those that are dark black verses the light brown. I submit to you that all of us have been brainwashed, bamboozled. Take a moment and picture the face of Jesus. The shape of His face, His nose, lips, eye, the color of His hair, the texture and the color of His skin. Do you see Him in your mind's eye?

How many of you pictured a Jesus that looks something like this? Even though I know that Jesus does not look like this, I still see this face in my mind's eye when I think of Jesus. You and I have been brainwashed to believe a lie. This is not a picture of Jesus. He DOES NOT look anything like this and we will prove that in session two with scripture.

Next, we will see a video entitled, "Cesare Borgia." Who is he and why is it important? Let us find out.

CESARE BORGIA

If this video link is no longer available, search by the video name.
(View this YouTube video link) https://youtu.be/kbIAzdnTxsU

How many of you saw a Jesus that looks something like this? That is one of the main reasons why the awakening is so important. If you are somewhat like me, as a child, I grew up with the pictures of a white Jesus. Some people say color doesn't matter, then why has one group of people gone to such extreme lengths to plaster an untruth image of our Messiah to the entire world?

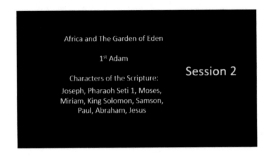

Africa and The Garden of Eden

1st Adam

Characters of the Scripture:
Joseph, Pharaoh Seti 1, Moses,
Miriam, King Solomon, Samson,
Paul, Abraham, Jesus

Session 2

Where did Civilization Begin?

Research on African history, European history and the Bible which gives credence to the fact that civilization began in Africa, where the black nations, including the Hebrew people, were the original inhabitants.

One erroneous deception that has been placed before us, for throughout history, has been the depiction of the continent of Africa. The Media always shows Africa in a negative light with little starving children living in deplorable conditions. Well, let us take a real look.

DECEPTION

USA   **AFRICA**

USA- It's epic, It's powerful, It's white! Therefore, it must be right! Compared to the little continent of Africa……. Much smaller, much weaker, full of salvages, only 3/5 of a human. Right? Wrong! Let us take a look.

TRUTH

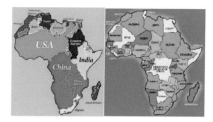

This Graphic shows Africa is as big as 13 nations and Eastern Europe. Do you see the actual size of USA compared to Africa? USA is MUCH smaller than Africa,

Note that Egypt, the so called Middle East is actually in Africa

The Sahara Desert- the largest desert in the world nearly as large as the USA

The Pharaonic civilization of ancient Egypt is one of the world's oldest and longest lasting civilization.

Africa's continent is the world's oldest populated area. The population will more than double to 2.3 billion people by the year 2050. There are fewer people with internet connection in African than there is in New York City.

Africa is the world's second largest continent covering more than 50 million square kilometers. It has approximately 30% of the earth's remaining mineral resources. It also has the largest reserve of precious metals with over 40% of gold reserves, over 60% of cobalt, and 90% of the platinum reserves.

Africa straddles the equator and is the only continent to extend from the northern temperate zone to the southern temperate zone. Africa is the hottest continent on earth. The average temperature is 93 degrees.

Victoria Falls is the largest waterfall in Africa; it is 355 feet high and one mile wide. Is this beautiful?

Madagascar is the largest island in Africa and the fourth largest island in the world. It is in the Indian Ocean off the East coast of Africa.

Mount Kilimanjaro is the highest mountain on the continent. It towers over 19,300 feet, which is so tall that glaciers can be found at its summit even though the mountain is near the equator. Africa is home to the largest living land animal, the elephant, which weighs up to 7 tons.

Next, we will see a video entitled, "Top 10 Most Livable cities in Africa 2016." If you have never been to Africa, this video will show you there are beautiful cities there. It is not just jungle and animals.

TOP 10 MOST LIVABLE CITIES IN AFRICA 2016

If this video link is no longer available, search by the video name.
(View this YouTube video link) https://youtu.be/FrLtfeXshQ4

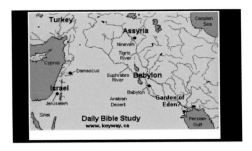

The Garden of Eden is described in the Bible as a wonderful and beautiful place and the original home of man.

> *"Now the LORD God had planted a garden in the east, in Eden; and there he put the man he had formed. And the LORD God made all kinds of trees grow out of the ground--trees that were pleasing to the eye and good for food. In the middle of the garden were the tree of life and the tree of the knowledge of good and evil. A river watering the garden flowed from Eden; from there it was separated into four headwaters. The name of the first is the Pishon;. . The name of the second river is the Gihon; . The name of the third river is the Tigris; . And the fourth river is the Euphrates."* **Genesis 2: 8-15**

Although we do not know the exact location of the Garden of Eden, we do know that the Tigris and Euphrates rivers are found in the countries of Iraq & Iran and thus near the Garden of Eden. Tradition has located Eden south of the ancient city of Ur in Iraq.

> *"⁷ And the LORD God formed man of the dust of the ground, and breathed into his nostrils the breath of life; and man became a living soul."* **Genesis 2:7 (KJV)**

Note: This is a game changer when it comes to perceiving the physical appearance of the ancient Hebrews because you automatically start off with an African humanity. It is no longer African appearance that needs to be explained in the light of the White Adam and Eve that grace the illustrated Bibles. It is now European appearance that needs explaining in the light of an original African Adam and Eve. Discovering the Garden of Eden in East Africa is also significant for another reason. This happens to be the region where the oldest fully human remains of the planet have been found. It is the region where **science meets the Bible**.

Next, we will see two videos entitled, "DNA Mystery the Search for Adam" and "National Geographic Forensic Scientist." Both videos will show you how science has proved that the first man, "Adam" was a black man. He was not white.

DNA MYSTERY THE SEARCH FOR ADAM

If this video link is no longer available, search by the video name.
(View this YouTube video link) https://youtu.be/LOMOoISOFyY

NATIONAL GEOGRAPHIC FORENSIC SCIENTIST

If this video link is no longer available, search by the video name.
(View this YouTube video link) https://youtu.be/Hz-GVwGsgDg

The question just changed. It is no longer, how did people of color get here? The question being asked now is, where did people with no Melanin come from? Now we realize that the Father & Mother of ALL people are black. The whole landscape has changed! What happened? How did it happen? Why did it happen? Some would say….it really doesn't matter. Why the cover up? Why have so many people for so long continued to cover up and hide the truth? Why is it still today, when we think of biblical characters, we picture persons different than what scripture and science teaches? It is one thing for others to keep the trust hidden from us but it is an atrocity when we do likewise! Wake up! It is time for us to wake up and get up! What did the biblical characters actually look like? We do not know for sure, but the following depictions are truer than what was presented previously. The following pictures are a more accurate depiction of what these major biblical characters looked like.

Joseph Brothers thought he was an Egyptian.

Let us take a look at Joseph and his time in Egypt. He was one of the twelve sons of Jacob and Joseph was clearly his favorite son. His brothers were jealous and ultimately their jealousy resulted in Joseph being sold to Arab merchants as a slave. Over the course of time, Joseph became the Governor of Egypt and was second in command to Pharaoh in authority. There was a famine in Canaan where Jacob and his sons lived. Pharaoh had a dream which Joseph interpreted. His dream told of the forthcoming famine and gave Egypt time to prepare by storing food. So, Jacob sent his ten sons to Egypt to buy bread.

Joseph was the governor of the land, the person who sold grain to all its people. So, when Joseph's brothers arrived, they bowed down to him with their faces to the ground. As soon as Joseph saw his brothers, he recognized them, but he pretended to be a stranger and spoke harshly to them.

> *"Where do you come from?" he asked. "From the land of Canaan,"*
> *they replied, "to buy food." Although Joseph recognized his brothers,*
> *they did not recognize him.* **Genesis 42 1-8**

Joseph's brother did not recognize him. They thought he was an Egyptian not an Israelite. He looked just like the Egyptians. You could not tell them apart.

Joseph's Image on a Coin

Coins found in Egypt Bearing the Name and Image of Joseph

This image of Joseph was found on **a coin in the land of Egypt**. According to the article, the back of the coin had images of **wheat and corn**. As governor of Egypt. Joseph's name appears twice on the coin, written in hieroglyphs. Once the original name, Joseph, and once his Egyptian name, Saba Sabani, which was given to him by the Pharaoh when he became treasurer.

A group of Egyptian researchers and archeologists has discovered coins from the time of the Pharaohs. The researchers discovered the coins when they sifted through thousands of small archeological artifacts stored in the vaults of the Museum of Egypt. They initially took them for charms, but a thorough examination revealed that the coins bore the year in which they were minted and their value.

Seti the first Pharaoh during the time of Moses

Seti 1 Pharaoh during the time of Moses

Truth   Deception

Many Scholars say the Pharaoh who was on the throne of Egypt at the time of Moses's birth was Pharaoh Seti the first. He was the father of Rameses 11. George Rawlinson, an English author, wrote a book entitled, "History of Egypt" on page 252 he gives a description of Seti the first. "Seti's face was thoroughly African. He had a stormy face with a depressed flat nose, thick lips, and heavy chin."

Could Moses look like this if Seti the first looked like this?

Now, let us take a look at the greatest and most famous story about the Israelites in the land of Egypt and Moses. Many years after the death of Joseph, his brothers and the entire generation entered Egypt during the time he was Governor. The Hebrews' population in Egypt grew tremendously. Because of this, they were no longer looked upon as friendly neighbors, the Egyptians now considered them hostile enemies and enslaved them. Because of the Hebrews population growth, the Egyptians decided they would impose upon them their own form of birth control. Pharaoh made a decreed that all Hebrew baby boys were to be killed at birth.

> *"And Pharaoh charged all his people, saying, every son that is born ye shall cast into the river, and every daughter ye shall save alive."*
> **Exodus 1:22**

Pharaoh was an Egyptian, a black man. Moses was a Hebrew, a black baby. No way would Moses have been able to grow up in Pharaoh's house for 40 years and Pharaoh not recognize that he was a Hebrew. Moses was born a Hebrew – Israelite from the tribe of Levi.

Moses and a Midianites Daughter

"Now a priest of Midian had seven daughters, and they came to draw water and fill the troughs to water their father's flock. ¹⁷ Some shepherds came along and drove them away, but Moses got up and came to their rescue and watered their flock. When the girls returned to Reuel (Jethro) their father, he asked them, why have you returned so early today? They answered, An <u>Egyptian</u> rescued us from the shepherds. He even drew water for us and watered the flock." **Exodus 2: 16-19**

Notice they did not say a Hebrew in Egyptian clothing saved us; instead, they described Moses as a black-skinned descendant of Ham (Egyptian).

A SURE sign for Moses

"Then the LORD said, put your hand inside your cloak. So, Moses put his hand into his cloak, and when he took it out, the skin was leprous—it had become as white as snow. Now put it back into your cloak, he said. So Moses put his hand back into his cloak, and when he took it out, it was restored, like the rest of his flesh. Then the LORD said, if they do not believe you or pay attention to the first sign, they may believe the second." **Exodus 4:6-8**

All the movies show you the first sign of the staff turning into a snake (we are all familiar with that sign) but the movies don't show you the 2ⁿᵈ sign which is a SURE way to prove without a shadow of doubt that God sent Moses. What would be the miracle of Charleston Hesston turning his white hand whiter? That would not be a great sign. If he were white, why not turn the hand black to be a sure sign of his miraculous power?

Aaron and his sister Miriam BEFORE Leprosy

"The anger of the LORD burned against them, and he left them. When the cloud lifted from above the tent, Miriam's skin was leprous—it became as white as snow. Aaron turned toward her and saw that she had a defiling skin disease." **Numbers12:9-10**

They spoke against Moses Ethiopian wife not because she was black but because she was from another nation. If Miriam was already white, why not turn her jet black. If she was white, there would not have been a punishment to turn her whiter.

Aaron and his sister Miriam AFTER Leprosy

Imagine you are talking to your ebony sister and you blink and SHE CHANGED RIGHT BEFORE YOUR EYES and this is what you see!!! How would you look? OMG, his eyes must have bucked out of his head!

King Solomon describes himself

"Dark am I, yet lovely, daughters of Jerusalem, dark like the tents of kedar, like the tent curtains of Solomon. Do not stare at me because I am dark, because I am darkened by the sun. My mother's sons were angry with me and made me take care of the vineyards; my own vineyard I had to neglect." **Songs of Solomon 1:5-7**

This is King Solomon describing his own complexion.

King Solomon's Locks

"All the days of his vow of separation there shall no razor come upon his head; until the days be fulfilled, in which he separated himself unto Jehovah, he shall be holy; he shall let the locks of the hair of his head grow long." **Numbers 6:5**

"And Delilah said unto Samson, Hitherto thou hast mocked, me, and told me lies; tell me wherewith thou mightiest be bound. And he said unto her, if thou weavest the seven locks of my head with the web." **Judges 16:13**

Straight hair never locks, but African American hair will naturally lock if it is not combed and allowed to grow. It will naturally grow into 7 locks.

Paul can speak Greek

"As the soldiers were about to take Paul into the barracks, he asked the commander, May I say something to you? Do you speak Greek?

He replied, Aren't you the Egyptian who started a revolt and led four thousand terrorists out into the wilderness some time ago? Paul answered, I am a Jew, from Tarsus in Cilicia, a citizen of no ordinary city. Please let me speak to the people." **Acts 21:37-39**

If Paul was a white man that spoke Greek, there would have been no mistake, the man would have simply thought Paul was Greek. In order for the chief captain to mistake Paul (the Hebrew) for a black skinned Egyptian, Paul had to look like an Egyptian. Once again we see in scripture that it was hard to tell a Hebrew from an Egyptian.

Abraham from Ur of the Chaldeans

We know that Abraham was black because he was born in the city founded by the black Nimrod, the grandson of Ham. The Bible dictionary defines Ham, Cush and Nimrod as black men.

> *"And there came one that had escaped, and told Abram the Hebrew;...... Abraham the first Hebrew was a descendent from Shem."* **Genesis 14:13 (KJV)**

Abraham came from Ur of the Chaldeans which is in the country of Iraq today. Genesis 11:31. **Godfrey Higgins a reliable English antiquary said, "The Chaldeans were originally Negros." Professor Rudolph Winsor is in total agreement with this which he states in his very not worthy book "From Babylon To Timbuktu", "The Chaldeans and other people of that region were jet black in their complexion."**

Abraham is the founding patriarch (father) of the Israelites, Ishmaelites, Edomites, and the Midianites and kindred peoples, according to the book of Genesis.

Review: The 12 tribes of Israel from the linage of Abraham. Jesus was born in the linage of Judah. (Abraham, Isaac, and Jacob)

Lineage of Jesus

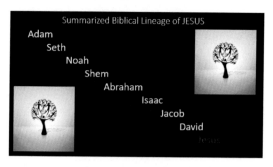

Jesus hiding in Egypt

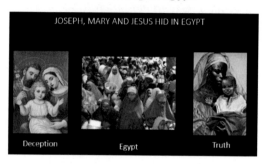

"The angel of the Most High told Joseph to arise and take the young child Yahshua (the Messiah's true Hebrew name) and his mother Mary (Miriam) and flee into Egypt." **Matthew 2:13**

He was told to stay there until he received further instructions because **Herod would seek the young child to kill him.**

They went to Egypt, but not for military protection. During this time, Egypt was a Roman province under Roman control. They fled into Egypt because Egypt was still a black country populated by a majority of black skinned people (Egyptians). Joseph, Miriam and Yahshua would have been just another black skinned family among many. Now why would they have fled into Egypt if they didn't look like them.

Biblical description of Jesus

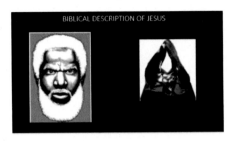

*"And his head and **his hair** were white as white **wool**, white as snow; and his eyes were as a flame of fire and **his feet like unto burnished brass, as if it had been refined in a furnace;** and his voice as the voice of many waters."* **Revelation 1:14-15**

*"I beheld till thrones were placed, and one that was ancient of days did sit; his raiment was white as snow, and the **hair of his head like pure wool**; his throne was fiery flames, and the wheels thereof burning fire."* **Daniel 7:9**

*"His body also was like the berly, and his face as the appearance of lightning, and his eyes as flaming torches, and **his arms and his feet like unto burnished brass**, and the voice of his words like the voice of a multitude."* **Daniel 10:6**

*"And to the angel of the church in Thyatira write: These things saith the Son of God, who hath is eyes like a flame of fire, and **his feet are like unto burnished brass.**"* **Revelation2:18**

If Jesus' hair was wooly and skin like a burnished brass and He was from the African region where the average temperature is 93, then who is this?

Jesus or Cesare Borgia?

This is a false picture of Jesus Christ. The first painting of Christ was in the 6th century about 500 years after Jesus died. So, how did we get these images of Jesus? Cesare's father, Rodrigo Borgia became Pope Alexander VI under the Catholic Church elite. He hired Leonardo da Vinci to paint his son as Christ. They used this false image of Cesare as Christ, and they brought forth a false teaching, ceremonies, sacrifices and holidays all along with this image to deceive the people to believe this was an accurate portrayal of Christ.

Next, we will see a video entitled, "Cesare Borgia, the False Image of Jesus Christ."

CESARE BORGIA: THE FALSE IMAGE OF JESUS CHRIST

If this video link is no longer available, search by the video name.
(View this YouTube video link) https://youtu.be/-7Q4qTZBBm4

Next, we will see a video entitled, "What Did Jesus Really Look Like?" No one knows exactly what He looked like, but science has proven that He definitely did not look white.

WHAT DID JESUS REALLY LOOK LIKE

If this video link is no longer available, search by the video name.
(View this YouTube video link) https://youtu.be/p0s2n6CQno4

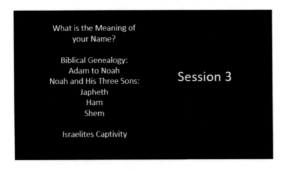

What is the Meaning of
your Name?

Biblical Genealogy:
Adam to Noah
Noah and His Three Sons:
Japheth
Ham
Shem

Israelites Captivity

Session 3

During Bible times, names were extremely important -- much more so then than now. Generations ago someone's name, not only designated who the person was, but **suggested the traits of the person.** For instance, the name Adam means human or earthling and comes from the Hebrew word that means earth or ground -- suggesting there was some correlation (like maybe being made from dust). Indeed, the word Adam is used throughout chapters two and three as a designation of "the human" and is not used as a name until Genesis 4:25. Thus, clearly the name Adam was used not only as an appellate, but also as a description of the person.

Next, we will see a video entitled, "Adam to Noah." It examines the meaning of names and how important the biblical names were. You will never look at these names the same again.

Also, if you do not already know, look up the meaning of your first name on the internet. You might find some interesting things about yourself. It is all in the name.

ADAM TO NOAH

If this video link is no longer available, search by the video name.
(View this YouTube video link) https://youtu.be/WkUdnsAA_kQ

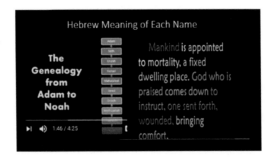

Hebrew Meaning of Each Name

The
Genealogy
from
Adam to
Noah

Mankind is appointed
to mortality, a fixed
dwelling place. God who is
praised comes down to
instruct, one sent forth,
wounded, bringing
comfort.

1:46 / 4:25

Mortality: Man will die.

Fixed dwelling place: Man lives on earth.

Comes down to instruct: Loving God...thought it not robbery to leave heaven and come to "earth"

One sent forth: By God / was God......while we were yet sinners, He came

Wounded: By us...verbally, beaten physically, hung on a tree...

Bringing comfort: IT IS FINISHED, BRINGING COMFORT!

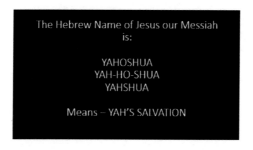

The Hebrew Name of Jesus our Messiah is:

YAHOSHUA
YAH-HO-SHUA
YAHSHUA

Means – YAH'S SALVATION

1611 King James Bible does not have the name Jesus. There is no letter "J" or "j" equivalent in the Hebrew language. As a matter of fact, the letter "J" is one of the last letters to be added to the English alphabet. The letter "J" came into widespread usage around the year 1630; there was no letter "J" in existence during biblical times. The letter "J" was created about 400 years ago and Jesus lived over 2000 years ago. There was not a letter "J" in Hebrew, Latin or Greek.

> *"And you shall know the truth and the truth shall make you free"*
> **John 8:32**

Scripture speaks to the fact that we would forget our Messiah's name.

> *"They think the dreams they tell one another will make my people forget my name, just as their ancestors forgot my name through Baal worship."* **Jeremiah 23:27**

All persons from Adam to Noah would have been from East Africa and would have been African.

The first generations of the genealogy of biblical figures occurs in the first book of the Bible, Genesis. The genealogies of Genesis record the descendants of Adam and Eve as given. Chapters four, five, and eleven report the lineal male descent to Abraham, including the age at which each patriarch fathered his named son and the number of years he lived thereafter. The genealogy for Cain is given in chapter four and the genealogy for Seth is in chapter five.

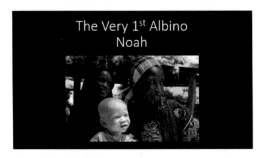

The Very 1st Albino
Noah

Noah was the very first "Albino" person born to the world. But pay attention to how his father, Lemech, describes him.

Book of Enoch,
> "After a time, my son Methuselah took a wife for his son Lamech. She became pregnant by him, and brought forth a child, the flesh of which was as white as snow, and red as a rose; the hair of whose head was white like wool, and long; and whose eyes were beautiful. When he opened them, he illuminated all the house, like the sun; the whole house abounded with light. And when he was taken from the hand of the midwife, opening also his mouth, he spoke to the Lord of righteousness. Then, Lamech his father was afraid of him; and flying away came to his own father Methuselah, and said, I have begotten a son, unlike to other children. He is not human; but, resembling the offspring of the angels of heaven, is of a different nature from ours, being altogether unlike to us. His eyes are bright as the rays of the sun; his countenance glorious, and he looks not as if he belonged to me, but to the angels. I am afraid, lest something miraculous should take place on earth in his days." **Chapter 105: 1-8**

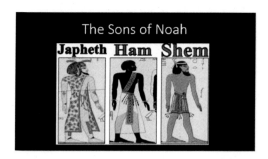

The Sons of Noah

The descendants of Noah appear in Genesis 10. The significance of Noah in this context is that, according to the Scripture, Genesis 6, was that a global flood destroyed all living things on the earth. God promised to never again cover the earth with water. The rainbow appeared in the sky as a sign of that promise. When we see it today, it reminds us of God's promise.

Japhetic refers to the descendants of Japheth, son of Noah. His genealogy is recorded in Genesis 10.

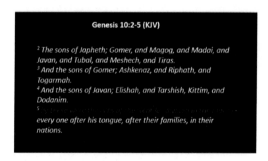

Genesis 10:2-5 (KJV)

[2] *The sons of Japheth; Gomer, and Magog, and Madai, and Javan, and Tubal, and Meshech, and Tiras.*
[3] *And the sons of Gomer; Ashkenaz, and Riphath, and Togarmah.*
[4] *And the sons of Javan; Elishah, and Tarshish, Kittim, and Dodanim.*
[5] *every one after his tongue, after their families, in their nations.*

The sons of Japheth are known as the Gentiles. Ashkenaz are from the lineage of Japheth. Hamitic refers to the descendants of Ham, son of Noah. **His genealogy is recorded in Genesis 10.**

Ham had four sons: Cush (Ethiopians/Cushites & Nubians); Mizraim (Egyptians & Khemet); Phut (Ancient Somalia) and Canaan (Canaanites the original inhabitants of the land of Israel).

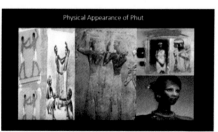

Physical Appearance of Canaan

Ham

The youngest son of Noah, born probably about 96 years before the Flood, and one of eight persons to live through the Flood. He became the progenitor of the dark races; not the Negroes, but the Egyptians, Ethiopians, Libyans and Canaanites.

Zondervan Compact Bible Dictionary

Most have been taught that all black people come from the seed of Ham, but once you research scholastic sources, the biblical scholars say something totally different. According to the Bible, there are only four families that made up the native population of Africa or the family of Ham: Egyptians, Ethiopians, Libyans and Canaanites, and the Negroes do not descend from any of them. In order to document this fact, extensive research has been done on both the native African and the so called Negro, which are two totally separate/different people as George M. Fredrickson, a Standford Professor, wrote in "The Black Image in the White Mind." In the 1840's Morton collaborated with George R. Gliddon, an Egyptologist, who provided him with mummy heads and information about the racial significance of Egyptian tomb inscriptions. In Crania Aegyptianca published in 1844, Morton pointed out that both cranial and archaeological evidence showed that the Egyptians were "NOT NEGROES."

He was trying to find out the racial origin of the American Negroes that were in slavery, so he compared skulls from the Egyptian tombs to the skulls of the American slaves. The Negro head was longer than the Egyptian head. They looked similar from the outside with the thick lips and broad nose, but once you start digging deeper, the differences were very noticeable.

Once he compared the skull of the slave in Egypt to the Negro, he found that the Negroes had in fact held the same servitude position in ancient Egypt as Americans.

So what does this mean? Could the American Negros be the same people as the biblical Israelites? Could they be the same people that were slaves in Egypt? Could they be the same people that God sent Moses to redeem from the hand of Pharaoh? The Bible tells us that slavery is a reoccurring theme for the Israelites. They cannot get away from slavery. It continues to happen over and over again even up until today because of disobedience.

So, if Ham is not the father of the Negros, who is? SHEM!

The sons of Shem can be found in Genesis 10:22-32. Semitic refers to the descendants of Shem, son of Noah. His genealogy is recorded in Genesis 10.

Nations drew depictions of themselves. They were dark complexions, (people of color) and they had kinky hair.

Pictures on the walls in Egypt.

> *"When the people saw that Moses delayed to come down from the mountain, the people gathered themselves together to Aaron and said to him, up, make us gods who shall go before us. As for this Moses, the man who brought us up out of the land of Egypt, we do not know what has become of him. So Aaron said to them, take off the rings of gold that are in the ears of your wives, your sons, and your daughters, and bring them to me."* **Exodus 32: 1-2**

The Israelite priest, wore earrings in their ears and bonnets on their heads.

> *"Then he brought Aaron's sons forward, put tunics on them, tied sashes around them and fastened caps on them, as the LORD commanded Moses."* **Leviticus 8:13**

Tunic is a cap (hemispherical bonnet)

> *"And the Lord spoke unto Moses, saying, speak unto the children of Israel and bid them that they make them fringes in the boarders of their garments throughout their generations."* **Numbers 15:37-38**

Girdle is a belt.

> *"The girdle was made of fine twined lined, of blue and purple and scarlet (RED) of needlework; as the Lord commanded Moses."* **Exodus 39:29**

Definition of *Nubian*. 1a: a native or inhabitant of *Nubia,* b: a member of one of the group of dark-skinned peoples that formed a powerful empire between Egypt and Ethiopia from the 6th to the 14th centuries.

Now, we will look at the Israelites going into one captivity after another because of their disobedience to God.

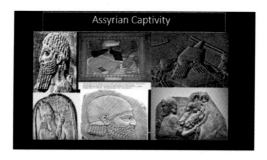

The Assyrians drew depictions of themselves. They were dark complexions and they had kinky hair. These were the first people to come in to conquer Israel and send them into captivity, 722 B.C.

> *"In the 9th year of Hoshea the king of Assyria took Samaria and carried Israel away into Assyria. This disaster came upon the people of Israel because they worshiped other deities. They sinned against God who had brought them safely out of Egypt and had rescued them from the power of Pharaoh, the king of Egypt."* **2Kings 17:6**

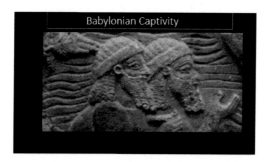

Then they came out of the land of Assyria and went back to the land of Israel, then the Babylonians (the modern day Ethiopians, Cushite's) came and made the Israelites slaves, 586 B.C.

> *"So, All Israel was reckoned by genealogies and behold they were written in the book of the kings of Israel and Judah, who were carried away to Babylon for their transgressions. 70 years of captivity under Babylon."* **1 Chronicles 9:1**

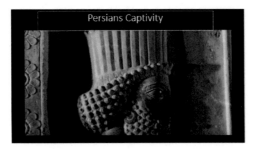

After the Babylonian captivity, the Israelites were captured by the Persians and put into slavery, 536 B.C.

> *"For we were bondmen, yet our God hath not forsaken us in our bondage, but hath extended mercy unto us in the sight of the kings of Persia."* **Ezra 9:9**

After the Persian captivity, then the Israelites were captured by the Greeks, 332 B.C.

> *"And to in treat them that they would take the yoke from them, for they saw that the kingdom of the Grecians did oppress Israel with servitude."* **1 Maccabees 8:18**

Romans Captivity

After the Greek captivity, 63 B.C., the Romans put Israel into slavery during the time of Christ.

Jeremiah 2:14

Is Israel a servant?
Is he a home born slave?
Why is he spoiled?

Israel was in slavery so often that Jeremiah had to ask, "Is Israel just put on this earth to be a slave? To serve other nations?" So, you might be asking yourself, if the Negros in America are part of the 12 tribes of Israel, how did the Israelites get to the West coast of Africa?

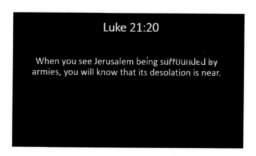

Luke 21:20

When you see Jerusalem being surrounded by armies, you will know that its desolation is near.

Christ was speaking to the Israelites and telling them that the Romans were going to destroy Israel.

Christ said when you see the Romans coming in, you get out and go to the mountains. The mountains that he was talking about was the land of Africa. The same place that Mary and Joseph took baby Jesus when they fled from Herod.

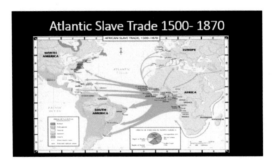

Atlantic Slave Trade 1500- 1870

A foreshadowing of the slave trade.

> "With cunning they conspire against your people; they plot against those you cherish. Come they say, let us destroy them as a nation, so that Israel's name is remembered no more. With one mind they plot together they form an alliance against you." **Psalm 83:3-5**

> "You sold the people of Judah and Jerusalem to the Greeks, that you might send them far from their homeland." **Joel 3:6**

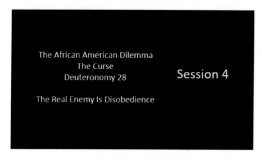

God's Chosen People

The fact that the Hebrews are God's chosen people means that they have been held to a higher standard.

> "And to whom so ever much is given, of him shall much be required and to whom they commit much, of him will they ask more." **Luke 12:48**

> "You only have I chosen of all the families of the earth; therefore I will punish you for all your sins." **Amos 3:2**

Are we living under the curse? Is it the white man's fault? They enslaved us! Is it the Black man's fault? They sold us into slavery! Whose fault is it? This is a "VICTIM" mentality. We cannot continue to blame others. We must take ownership of where we are and how we got here.

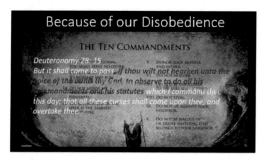

Take note of what God is saying here in Deuteronomy 28:15; these curses are to be used as a sign. God gave us these signs, so that the true Israelite COULD be identified, not hidden. Let us consider something for a moment.

Let us say you had no idea what a **duck** looked like, but someone told you to be on the lookout for one. As a matter of fact, the person telling you to watch for a duck had never seen one either. But, they had been given this **description: an aquatic bird, with a long neck, a flat bill, scaled legs, webbed feet, short rounded body, waddles when walking and makes a quacking sound.**

Now that you have a description, though you have never seen a duck, you would know that a **horse is NOT a duck, nor is a dog or a cat.** Now you may have a **problem if a geese or swan came your way,** but you could at least tell these animals are in the same family.

In the same way the true nation of Israel can be identified today, all 12 tribes are all still around, and they still have the signs/curses upon them for not obeying their God.

They MUST have them, for we will soon see that the nation of Israel, as a whole, did NOT obey God. Some of the tribes you may be able to recognize immediately, others may be harder to identify. But, one thing is for certain, with the signs/curses given to us in God's holy Word, you will definitely be able to tell who is NOT of the seed of Israel!

Here is something else to consider, if you have a people that claim to be a certain people, but have NONE of the signs/curses upon them or their seed as the Lord said, "Who do you believe?" God's holy Word…..or the ones making the claim?

For those reading, please understand: God's signs/curses are upon a nation of PEOPLE…..NOT a nation, as in the US, Germany or Spain. So, in whatever nation any of the 12 tribes of Israel finds herself, God's curses will be upon her. As we will soon read, the nation where Israel dwells may prosper and all the people around Israel may prosper, but God tells us NOT ISRAEL!

Let us read God's holy Word and find out the truth. God gave us these signs so, ALL that read will know who are the true Israelites. Let us read the curses and also find out if Israel kept or rejected God's laws. For if we find that they **did NOT keep God's laws** and commandments, we can write off ALL of the blessings that were to be bestowed unto them.

Let us go with just the Word of God on this one. Man and his history are not always true…but God's Word NEVER lies!

RELATIONSHIP/COVENANT. God made a covenant with Israel and all Israel's descendants when He brought them out of Egypt. In Deuteronomy 28:1-14 you will find the blessing, but it is conditional. God will bless if Israel would diligently hearken to the voice of God. In Deuteronomy 28:15-68, you will find the curses if Israel did not diligently hearken to the voice of God.

If you read Deuteronomy 29:9-14, you will see that God made a covenant with the present Israel who were physically present during this covenant and future generations of Israelites not present. Those who are not here today, (future generations)

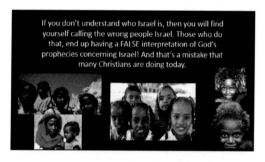

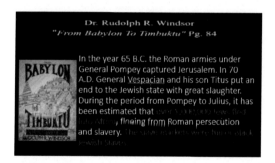

They were running from the Roman solders because they were going to slaughter the Israelites. The ones that didn't leave, that didn't take heed to the prophecy when they got caught by the Romans were taken back to Europe and put into slavery and became gladiators. Others who listened had no choice but to migrate to Africa where Rome had no jurisdiction.

"The children also of Judah and the children of Jerusalem have ye sold unto the Grecians, that ye might remove them far from their border. The Africans sold Israelites to the Grecians/Europeans into slavery." **Joel 3:6**

The Israelites did not assimilate with the local African population see page 90 of Babylon Timbuktu.

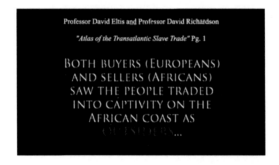

Now, why was that? Because they were selling another nation who had migrated into their territory encroaching on their land. A different nation with different customs. The Africans had no problem selling the Israelites into slavery. The Africans DID NOT sell their own people. This is an untruth that has been written in the European textbooks.

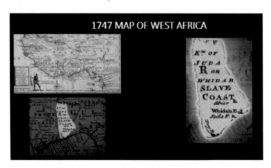

Called by His Name

Search the internet for the slave voyages and look for the slaves that had Yahshua as part of their name. Notice in this one search, there are 822 slaves with Yah as a part of their name. Is this coincidental?

> *"If my people, who are called by my name, shall humble themselves, and pray, and seek my face, and turn from their wicked ways; then will I hear from heaven, and will forgive their sin, and will heal their land."* **2 Chronicles 7:14**

Next, we will see a video entitled "Curses of Deuteronomy 28" This video will show you how closely the slave trade lines up with Scripture. There are no coincidents or "happen stances" with God. He knows everything.

CURSES OF DEUTERONOMY 28

If this video link is no longer available, search by the video name.
(View this YouTube video link) https://youtu.be/crWFMHh-LkY

- What stood out to you in this video clip?
- How do you feel about what you saw?
- Is Deuteronomy 28 speaking to the state of the African American people? Why or why not?

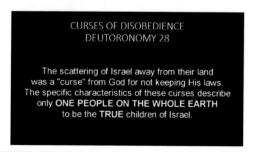

> God said ALL of His curses would fall upon ALL of the nation of Israel and ALL of her SEED if they did not obey Him. That would be ALL 12 tribes! That means God's curses are STILL on ALL of Israel's seed TODAY! God gave us these signs, so that the world may KNOW who are the true Israelites and who are NOT!

Take note of what God is saying. These curses are to be used as a sign. God gave us these signs, so the true Israelite COULD be identified, not hidden. Let us consider something for a moment.

> The Hebrews, the Israelites, are the chosen people of God.
>
> *6 For you are a holy people to the LORD your God; the LORD your God has chosen you to be a people for Himself, a special treasure above all the peoples on the face of the earth.* ~**Deuteronomy 7:6 (NKJV)**

> For what reason were they chosen?
>
> - God wanted citizens of His Kingdom living on earth in a manner that expressed His love for them and their love and commitment to Him and all of humankind.
> - To the point that other nations would see and join God's Kingdom through His Son Jesus The Christ!

The Cover UP

Ashkenazi Jews Influence on:
books, media, television, movies

White Washed

Session 5

Willie Lynch Letter

Stolen Identity

A STOLEN IDENTITY

Scripture prophesied that the children of Israel would be cut off from being a nation of people because there would be a calculated plan, scheme, a deliberate attempt to destroy God's people.

> "The have taken crafty counsel against thy people, and consulted against thy hidden ones. They have said, come and let us cut the off from being a nation; that the name of Israel may be no more in remembrance. For they have consulted together with one consent; they are confederate against thee." **Psalm 83:3-5**

> "According as it is written, God hath given them the spirit of slumber, eyes that they should not see, and ears that they should not hear; unto this day." **Romans 11:8**

> "The ox knows his owner, and the ass his master's crib but Israel doth not know, my people doth not consider." **Isaiah 1:3**

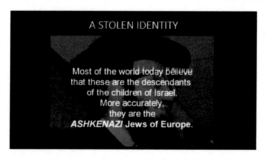

A STOLEN IDENTITY

Most of the world today believe that these are the descendants of the children of Israel. More accurately, they are the *ASHKENAZI* Jews of Europe.

The European Ashkenazi Jews simply DO NOT fit the curse of Deuteronomy 28. They are not oppressed as a people, they control Hollywood (movies), the media (news and publication companies), banks (Federal Reserve) and played a great roll in the slave traders, and they have not been TAKEN all over the world as slaves. The bible states when the real Jews are in Israel, there will be peace. Is there peace in Israel now?

They converted to Judaism during the 8th and 9th Century. The Holocaust, which was politically motivated, was used by the Elite to invade the land of Israel and placed the Kazarians in the land in 1948.

Ashkenazi is a German word that describes German descent. That is why they speak "Yiddish," a German language mixed with Hebrew. Biblical Israelites are not descendants of Europe. They can also be traced back to the Kazarian tribes of Russia prior to migration to Germany.

If these are God's chosen people. Why aren't all the 12 tribes of Israel back in the Holy Land right now? Why is God allowing them to have the largest gay pride parade every year for the last 15 years? Why is God allowing 3 major religions to be worshipped in Jerusalem? Catholic, Islam, and Judaism. Why is there war and not peace in Jerusalem?

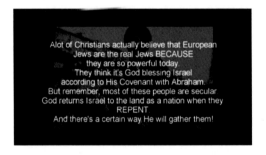

Alot of Christians actually believe that European Jews are the real Jews BECAUSE they are so powerful today. They think it's God blessing Israel according to His Covenant with Abraham. But remember, most of these people are secular. God returns Israel to the land as a nation when they REPENT And there's a certain way He will gather them!

"In that day the Root of Jesse will stand as a banner for the peoples; the nations will rally to him, and his resting place will be glorious. In that day the Lord will reach out his hand a second time to reclaim the surviving remnant of his people from Assyria, from Lower Egypt, from Upper Egypt, from Cush, from Elam, from Babylonia, from Hamath and from the islands of the Mediterranean. He will raise a banner for the nations and gather the exiles of Israel; he will assemble the scattered people of Judah from the four quarters of the earth. Ephraim's jealousy will vanish, and Judah's enemies[d] will be destroyed; Ephraim will not be jealous of Judah, nor Judah hostile toward Ephraim." **Isaiah 11:10-13**

Did God say in 1948 that the United Nations would gather Israel as a nation? Or did He say the Lord would gather Israel as a nation? In 1948, the state of Israel was created and many Europeans were flown to Israel and took on the identity of Jews. How could this happen? Easily because true Israel fled the land and forgot their identity, so it was free for the taking and the imposters took hold of an identity, but not the promise. God's word is true.

One of the places the Messiah will gather true Israelites is from Cush/Ethiopia. So real Jews should be in Ethiopia today. The only Jews in Ethiopia are black!

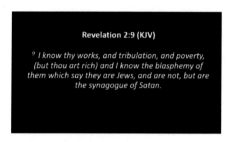

This is what Jesus said about the Jews.

"You shall know the truth and the truth shall set you free." **John 8:32**

Who controls a lot of the music? The music that our youth listen to, such as rap music that has an agenda that is being pushed on our youth and music about violence, sex, and drugs.

Who controls the largest news outlets, where we get so-called reliable news information? Who decides what the top stories are? Who decides what is important to the readers? **THE JEWS.**

Next, we will see a video entitled "How white people changed the identity of Biblical Characters." I think that is self-explanatory. Let us take a look at the video.

HOW WHITE PEOPLE CHANGED THE IDENTITY OF BIBLICAL CHARACTERS

If this video link is no longer available, search by the video name.
(View this YouTube video link) https://youtu.be/7FhgNHc6HW4

The next three videos will show how reporters have been selective on what is important when it comes to deaths in America. Mostly the news will be weighted toward making white look right such as **Selective Reporting**. News is supposed to be unbiased, but is it?

QUANELL X AND MATT PATRICK FACE OFF RE 9 11 & BLACK WALL STREET

If this video link is no longer available, search by the video name.
(View this YouTube video link) https://youtu.be/RklFKVT87EQ

HELL ON WHEELS CHIEF VS US

If this video link is no longer available, search by the video name.
(View this YouTube video link) https://youtu.be/abVfe2upuTl

WILLIE LYNCH 'THE MAKING OF A SLAVE'

If this video link is no longer available, search by the video name.
(View this YouTube video link) https://youtu.be/PcXWr-6SQqE

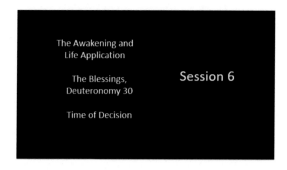

The Awakening and
Life Application

The Blessings,
Deuteronomy 30

Session 6

Time of Decision

The Black Church – Why is it that Sunday is still the most segregated day of the week? God has not let us become totally comfortable in the Christianity white America forced on us during slavery. It appears that He is keeping us segregated for such a time as this when we begin worshipping Him as the true God and obeying Him with our heart and soul according to His word.

Israelites are waking up all over the world by the thousands. Getting rid of these Gentile gods and coming back to the most-high God, the creator of heaven and earth and keeping their end of the covenant. The kingdom of heaven (ruler ship), the governing body is being set up right now in the midst of everyone and nobody even knows it. While America is on economic decline, God is raising up the ruling government of the Kingdom of Heaven.

Read the actual scripture below of **Deuteronomy 30:1-10** and then view the video entitled "Black Future/Israel's Return from Captivity." This video summarizes the Trans-Atlantic Slave Trade and then goes directly into Deuteronomy 30 which is the promise of God, the good news.

Prosperity After Turning to the Lord

> *"When all these blessings and curses I have set before you come on you and you take them to heart wherever the Lord your God disperses you among the nations, and when you and your children return to the Lord your God and obey Him with all your heart and with all your soul according to everything I command you today, then the Lord your God will restore your fortunes and have compassion on you and gather you again from all the nations where He scattered you. Even if you have been banished to the most distant land under the heavens, from there the Lord your God will gather you and bring you back. He will bring you to the land*

that belonged to your ancestors, and you will take possession of it. He will make you more prosperous and numerous than your ancestors. The Lord your God will circumcise your hearts and the hearts of your descendants, so that you may love Him with all your heart and with all your soul, and live. The Lord your God will put all these curses on your enemies who hate and persecute you. You will again obey the Lord and follow all His commands I am giving you today. Then the Lord your God will make you most prosperous in all the work of your hands and in the fruit of your womb, the young of your livestock and the crops of your land. The Lord will again delight in you and make you prosperous, just as He delighted in your ancestors, if you obey the Lord your God and keep His commands and decrees that are written in this Book of the Law and turn to the Lord your God with all your heart and with all your soul." **Deuteronomy 30:1-10**

BLACK FUTURE / ISRAEL'S RETURN FROM CAPTIVITY

If this video link is no longer available, search by the video name. (View this YouTube video link) https://youtu.be/f6681IM_cmA

In Conclusion

Will you share this life changing information with others? Many people are drowning in this process we call life, simply because they do not have a true identity. The identity they have been given does not fit according to scripture. God has sustained your true history in the world's most famous book, our history book; the Bible. Read it with new eyes and with a new heart to hear what God has to say to you. God is calling His chosen people to come back to our first love. God is our first love. We are to keep His commandments, obey Him, and by returning to God's Word, He will reveal Himself to us according to His Word.

We have prayed for everyone reading The Awakening. Our prayer is that you have accepted Jesus Christ, Yahshua as your Lord and Savior. At the end of the day, only what we do for Christ will last. Experiencing The Awakening has been a labor of love for us but our ultimate goal is to help those seeking to find their true identity in Jesus Christ, Yahshua. If you have not accepted

Jesus, we invite you to be saved and accept Jesus as your Lord and Savior today, which is as simple as ABC:

> **A – Admit** you are a sinner. **Romans 3:23** *"For all have sinned, and come short of the glory of God."*

> **B – Believe** in your heart that God has raised Jesus from the dead. . **John 14:6** *"Jesus saith unto him, I am the way, the truth, and the life: no man cometh unto the Father, but by me."* **Hebrews 11:6** *"But without faith it is impossible to please Him; for he that cometh to God must believe that He is, and that He is a rewarder of them that diligently seek Him."*

> **C – Confess** your sins. **Romans 10:10** *"For with the heart man believeth unto righteousness; and with the mouth confession is made unto salvation."* **Romans 10:9** *"That if thou shalt confess with thy mouth the Lord Jesus, and shalt believe in thine heart that God hath raised him from the dead, thou shalt be saved."* **Romans 10:13** *"For everyone who calls on the name of the Lord, will be saved."*

A Prayer of Commitment

Dear Lord, I know I am a sinner and I need Your forgiveness. I believe that You died for my sins. I want to turn from my sins. I now invite You to come into my heart and life. I want to trust and follow You as Lord and Savior in Jesus' name, Amen.

You probably have tried everything else, why not try Jesus Christ! You have nothing to lose, but Eternity to gain.

The first step toward getting somewhere is to decide that you are not going to stay where you are.

If you want your dreams to come true, the first thing you have to do is WAKE UP!

REFERENCES

Books
- Bible
- From Babylon To Timbuktu by Rudolph R. Windsor
- Encyclopedia of the Jewish Diaspora Origins, Experiences, and Culture, Volumn 1 by Mark Avrum Ehrlich Professor of Judaic Studies
- Atlas of the Tranatlantic Slave Trade by Professor David Eltis and Professor David Richardson
- Black Jews in Africa and The Americas by Tudor Parfitt, Professor of Modern Jewish Studies
- Miseducation of the Negroes by Carter Godwin Woodson
- The Black Image in the White Mind by George M. Fredrickson a Stanford Professor
- The Truth About Black Biblical Hebrew-Israelites by Ella J. Hughley
- The Destruction of Black Civilization by Chancellor Williams

REFERENCES

Books
- The Hidden Treasure that Lies in Plain Sight by Jeremy Shorter
- White Like Me by Tim Wise
- The Ancient Black Hebrews and Arabs by Gert Muller, Anu M-Vantu
- The History of White People by Nell Irvin Painter
- The New Jim Crow by Michelle Alexander

REFERENCES

Videos:
- Proof Biblical Israelites were Black & Why it Does Matter (Standintall 43)
- Hidden Identity of Blacks in the Bible (Full Documentary) (Yosef)
- Biblical Israelites were Black and Still are Today (Jo El)
- True Biblical History – African Hebrew Israelites or Jews (Standintall 43)
- Who are the Real Biblical Israelites? (Truth Unveiled 777)
- The True Hebrew Israelites 100% Undeniable Proof the Bible is Real (Joseph Yah Ben Israel)
- Physical Appearance of the True Hebrew Israelites (Ncognito)
- Undeniable Proof the Jews are Black (Joseph Yah Ben Israel)
- The R.E.A.L. Talk – Undoing Racism in America's Cities
- The History of the Real Hebrew Israelites
- A History of the True Hebrews

REFERENCES

12. Phut=Samolians
13. Canaanites=original inhabitants of the land of Israel.
14. Gentile comes from the Hebrew word Goy, which means nation.
15. Egypt – Land of Boundage
16. YAHOSHUA - -- YAH-HO-SUA ---YAHSUA (YAH'S SALVATION)
17. Yeshue – to rescue to deliver
18. Jesus – the letter "J" did not come into existence until early 1600. In June 1632 in a court of law in England, a printing company was being sued because they spelled Yeshua as Jesus. The spelling stuck and the rest is history.
19. Jewish people are referred to in Scripture as Jews, Israelites, Daughters of Zion, God's Chosen People, Hebrews, Children of Abraham.

REFERENCES

Books
- The Willie Lynch Letter and Making of a Slave by Willie Lynch
- The Black Presence In the Bible and the Table of Nations by Rev. Walter Arthur McCray
- The Complete Works of Blacks in the Bible by James H. Warden Jr.
- Creating Black Americans by Nell Irvin Painter
- Hebrews to Negroes by Ronald Dalton Jr.
- The Black Negro and the Black Christ by Aylmer Von Fleisher
- Wake up to your true Identity by Maurice Lindsay
- The Hidden Treasures that lie in plain sight by Jeremy Shorter
- The Souls of Black Folks by W. E. B. Du Bois
- The Rise and Fall of Black Wall Street by Robin Walker
- 100 Amazing Facts about Negros by J. A. Rogers

REFERENCES

Movie Clips
- Monkey Business Illusion
- A Time to Kill
- National Geographic ADAM
- Blacks are in fact the true Hebrews of the Bible
- Curse of Deuteronomy 28
- Quanell X and Matt Patrick Face Off 911 & Black Wall Street Bombing
- Hell on Wheels Chief vs US
- Willie Lynch Letter
- The Real Truth about Christopher Columbus
- The Physical Appearance of the True Hebrew Israelites
- From Adam to Noah
- What Did Jesus Really Look Like
- Black Future / Israel's Return From Captivity
- How white people changed the Identity of Biblical Characters
- Parents React To The UNIB Race Doll Test
- Top 10 best Cities in Africa 2016 HD
- The Truth About Black People (Haitians, Jamaicans and Africans)

REFERENCES

1. Bible is the History book of the Israelites
2. History can be distorted by the perspective of the writter
3. Genealogy shows the family lineage
4. Indigenous, aboriginal: people that has been in a region from the earliest time
5. God's Chosen People
6. Aberrancies are the original people of a land
7. Ham in Hebrew means hot, brunt or black
8. Cush=Kushites, Nubians and Ethiopians
9. Cush=Kushites, Nubians and Ethiopians
10. Ethiopian comes from the Greek work Aethiops which means brunt of black face. The Greeks applied this name to the Nubians and Kushites who lived south of the Egyptians.
11. Miziraim=Egyptian, Pathos, Kement and KMT

Acknowledgments

We would like to thank each of our friends for their encouragement during The Awakening journey with special acknowledgment to Rick Williams, Carolyn Harrison, Thomasena Gooden, Danita Ruth and Cherrel Jackson.

Made in the USA
San Bernardino, CA
22 April 2018